Instructions f

LET AUGMENTED REALITY CHAN

With your smartphone, iPad or tablet you can use the **Hasmark AR** app to invoke the augmented reality experience to literally read outside the book.

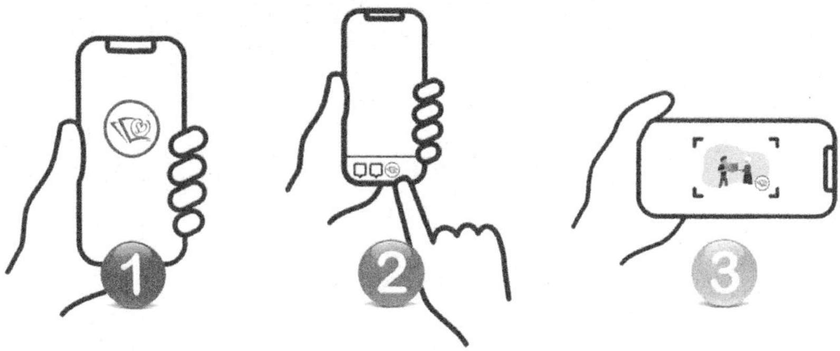

1. Download the **Hasmark app** from the **Apple App Store** or **Google Play**
2. Open and select the (vue) option
3. Point your lens at the full image with the and enjoy the augmented reality experience.

Go ahead and try it right now with the Hasmark Publishing International logo.

ENDORSEMENTS – RITA HAMILTON

This book is truly remarkable. Rita provides an incredible, raw, and honest account of childhood sexual trauma, and what a difficult journey healing from such experiences can be. It allows the reader to truly connect with the survivor and empathize with her pain, while also helping them understand the complex nature of this type of trauma. Extremely well written!

—**Jamie-Lynn Sluman** BA,
RSSW Psychotherapist.

Rita Hamilton has done a great service to humanity with *Nobody's Baby* by telling a sensitive and powerful story of the trauma of childhood sexual abuse through her daughter-in-law's voice. This book is essential reading for anyone who has children under their care, whether social workers, teachers, parents, family members, or neighbors. It brings awareness of the problem into sharp focus through the details of events of a girl's infancy through adulthood and her journey to obtain justice and ongoing healing.

—**Tressa Mitchener**,
Author of *Looking Out From the Inside*

Nobody's Baby is a riveting and insightful book that will give survivors of childhood sexual abuse the courage and inspiration to heal themselves from their emotional and psychological trauma.

—**Judy O'Beirn**,
International Bestselling Author

NOBODY'S *Baby*

RITA HAMILTON

Hasmark
PUBLISHING
INTERNATIONAL

Published by
Hasmark Publishing International
www.hasmarkpublishing.com

Second Edition

Editor: Jamie Geidel jamie@hasmarkpublishing.com
Cover Designer: Anne Karklins anne@hasmarkpublishing.com
Layout Artist: Amit Dey amit@hasmarkpublishing.com

ISBN 13: 978-1-77482-208-1
ISBN 10: 1774822083

Hasmark PUBLISHING INTERNATIONAL

DEDICATION

For Kassidy, Sadie, and Esmé,
my heart and soul.

THE DARKNESS

There are the bright, light days
when The Darkness crouches in the shadows,
never rearing its ugly head,
never whispering its miserable narratives in your ear,
when it allows you to live and laugh and love.

There are the cloudy days
when The Darkness follows along beside you,
holding your hand,
feigning a sick friendship and love,
a love that will devour you from the inside out,
if you let it.

There are the black, cold and damp days
when The Darkness grabs you by your wrists
and drags you into the bottomless well
of self doubt and guilt,
where it leaves you to claw your way out,
if you can.
You can.

TABLE OF CONTENTS

INTRODUCTION

This is Verity's story. It's a true story about child sexual and physical abuse and rape. It's a story about trauma and drug use, and it's a story about the effects of family abandonment and shunning on a person's mental health and self-worth. But most of all, it's a story about hope and recovery. About the human condition and our ability to rise above childhood trauma.

We are led to believe that our family, especially our mother, is our safe place, the place where we will be protected from evil, the place we can always run to when we're scared or hurt. Sadly, this is all too often not the case at all for child sexual abuse victims. In Verity's case, her mother served her up on a silver platter to her stepfather. Eventually, after she gained the courage and the maturity to report her stepfather to the police, she was harassed, called a liar, shunned, and abandoned by her whole family, even after her stepfather was convicted on all counts of sexually abusing her and five other little girls and was sent to prison.

Verity's biological father, whom she never met until she was twelve and again when she was sixteen, never instilled in her a feeling of worth or family inclusion that she unknowingly but so desperately needed. She managed to build a relationship with him, her stepmother, and her two half sisters as an adult after her first son was born. However, when she finally began her recovery journey, she had to be honest with herself and admit that the relationship was based on his need to ease his own conscience and on her own desperate search for a loving family. There was no real connection or genuine love. Those things that are cultivated and grown over time through shared experiences, family get-togethers, arguments, and laughs—these things were missing. As much as she tried to insert herself into the family unit, and as much as they tried to include her, it became painfully clear that she was an outsider and always would be.

When she went public and had her stepfather charged, the court dates and accusations that ensued were clearly too much for her newfound family. They distanced themselves from the court proceedings and the oh-so-difficult conversations about her childhood abuse. They didn't sign up for all of that. They wanted to do the right thing, but it was all too raw and hard and just plain uncomfortable.

Verity, as is the case with so many victims of child sexual abuse, developed Borderline Personality Disorder, Attachment Disorder, Anxiety Disorder, PTSD, and a serious addiction to drugs. It would be many years before she could even *begin* to understand how to love herself or anyone else in a healthy way.

Verity came to think of herself as "Nobody's Baby".

Please keep in mind when you read this account of child sexual abuse that this is not a rare or unique case. This is much more common than we want to believe. Know that there are many more victims out there who have fought and continue to fight every day to keep going and not give in to mental illness and addiction. Know that there are just as many who have lost their battle and their life. Every day children are abused and accused of seducing or encouraging their abuser. This is wrong. Children cannot consent to sex with an adult, and it is always the abuser who is at fault. This misguided and misplaced blame is killing children and contributing to generational trauma . . . It has to stop.

Verity and I sincerely hope that *Nobody's Baby* will help others in similar circumstances learn to love themselves. We hope they will come to believe that they are deserving of love and will find their way in this world believing that they are lovable.

PRESENT DAY

It's 6:00 a.m. Verity's husband has long since left for work when Verity is jolted awake by a hand on her shoulder and warm breath in her ear. She sits bolt upright in a full-on panic attack unable to catch her breath or speak. She's frozen in place and fear is gripping her heart like a vice threatening to cut off her oxygen and squeeze the very life blood from her veins.

"Mom, it's me." Twelve-year-old Benji, her baby, speaks calmly and quietly having been here with his mom many times before. "Sorry, I just wanted to find out if you know where my bike helmet is."

Verity turns to face the wall on the other side of the bed, forcing herself to breathe and read the list of steps to reduce anxiety and panic that her husband has posted there for her. A couple of minutes pass before she finally feels her heart begin to slow and her breathing start to regulate.

Benji stands near the bed, seemingly unphased, patiently waiting for his mom to respond. He scolds himself every time this happens because he knows what her PTSD triggers are, and he knows he should stand back and call her quietly to wake her up, but he is twelve, after all. "Sorry Mom," he says again.

Hearing the voices downstairs, fourteen-year-old Clinton soon appears in the doorway in full big brother mode, rubbing his eyes.

"Benj, what are doing down here? I told you where your bike helmet is. C'mon I'll show you again."

Verity smiles at Clinton and pulls Benji close, hugging him with everything she has. "It's okay, buddy, not your fault." She thinks, again, as she often does lately, that she must have been blessed with her two sweet boys, so much like their father, to make her see that not all men are evil.

THE OFFERING

In 1987 Verity's mother began cheating on Verity's biological father. She was having an affair with Verity's soon-to-be stepfather. Verity was around one month old when her mother, Evil-lyn, moved Verity's stepfather, Pedo, into their home and set the fateful trajectory of her life in motion.

She can't remember when she came to understand that Pedo wasn't her real dad, but she always thought of him as her dad in every sense of the word and loved him through all the abuse he inflicted upon her. And when she is being honest with herself, she will admit that she still loves him today. He was her "dad", and although he sexually abused and raped her from a very young age, her emotionally and psychologically damaged brain still has difficulty fully recognizing him for the monster he is. He was nice to her, he showed her affection that her mother never did, he told her he loved her, and as sick and depraved as it was, he made her feel good.

Evil-lyn was a physical, psychological, and emotional abuser, and in hindsight it is obvious to Verity that she was offered up to Pedo on a silver platter, so to speak. She often ponders why and how her mother could have done such a thing. It reminds her of the way a cat brings home a dead mouse and leaves it lovingly on the doorstep—a gift to show its master how much it loves him. It doesn't matter to the cat that the mouse was tortured and finally killed; it only matters that the cat has a gift to present to its master. Was Verity her mother's gift to

Pedo? She not only offered her up; she offered up all of the little girls that would visit their house alone or with their parents. Her heart still aches when she thinks about her mother knowing what Pedo was doing and not only being okay with it, but actually helping him, setting things up for him. Evil-lyn seemed to have a sick attachment to Pedo. He was not only a pedophile, abusing her own daughter, but he cheated on Evil-lyn more than once, even getting their seventeen-year-old babysitter pregnant. Still, she stood by him. It was like she needed him to feel better about herself. No matter how bad she felt about herself, he would always be worse in her eyes, and she would verbally beat him down the way a boxer takes out his frustrations on the punching bag. Between the lines of everything she said to him you could read, "Maybe I am a bad person, but you're so much worse than me."

When Verity's addictions were at their worst, she would spend most of her time thinking about the past and what happened to her, how her family turned their back on her, and what part of it all she was to blame for. She would think about Evil-lyn yelling and screaming at Pedo, berating him in front of their friends while he stood by saying nothing—a pathetic beaten little man. She can still recall the sympathy she felt for Pedo at those times. No one knew better than she did how it felt to have the wrath of Evil-lyn unleashed on you. She felt sorry for him, she loved him, and she hated him.

Later in life Verity discovered that Evil-lyn too had been sexually abused by her own uncle as a child. That same uncle raped his own two little girls, and his wife stood by him to the day he died. Perhaps this is where Evil-lyn learned her sick loyalty to Pedo. One day, after Verity had Pedo charged, she was visiting with her grandmother, and the conversation went to the uncle who had raped his two little girls. "They had it much worse than you did, Verity," Grandma quipped. How her grandma ever came to that conclusion still puzzles Verity today. Obviously, she too felt the need for some kind of redemption, telling herself that Verity's abuse "wasn't that bad."

Pedo was the neighbourhood "amazing dad" always more than happy to have the neighbourhood kids over on his days off for full days of games and fun. Pedo and his wife had a lot of friends, they were popular, and Pedo was happy, eager even, to have all the kids over to his house on his days off. It was common for parents to drop their kids off for Pedo to babysit on weekends and holidays, kind of like the neighbourhood fun house, in a ***lambs-to-the-slaughter*** sort of way.

Verity was just learning to dress herself, just three years old, when Evil-lyn started asking her in front of Pedo, "Do you want to sleep like mommy tonight, with no underwear?" Verity, always eager to impress her cold mother, wanted to do anything that might make her proud. The little girl would do anything for her mother, including, as it turned out, pleasure her husband. Little did she know that her mother would come to hate her for doing the very things she allowed and in fact encouraged. By the time Verity was nine, Evil-lyn had become the proverbial jealous wife, jealous of her own little girl.

Some would argue that Evil-lyn was even sicker than Pedo. Verity was her baby, just three years old, when she offered her up to her husband like another woman might offer her husband a nice dinner.

HOOKED ON THE FEELING

Verity was about three when Pedo started to sexually molest her, although it's hard to say for sure, as the human memory is unreliable when it comes to chronological detail. It could have been earlier.

She remembered Evil-lyn showing her how to take her underwear off and put it back on. She felt loved and doted on because she was allowed to sleep with daddy and mommy every night. Incredibly, Pedo sexually molested Verity every night even though Evil-lyn was right there in bed with them. Later in life Verity came to understand that her mother knew only too well what was going on and that this was the reason behind her encouraging her to sleep without underwear.

Almost instantly, Verity was hooked on the feeling she got from the orgasms. She couldn't get enough. She had no idea it was wrong in any way. How could it be wrong? Her daddy was doing it, and he loved her. He cuddled her and told her so all the time. He never hit her or yelled at her. In fact, the only parental affection in her life came from the man she thought of as her daddy. She was little more than a baby, and she was addicted to sex. She couldn't remember a single hug, kiss, or even a few words of verbal affection from her mother, and she was starving for it, as all children are. She needed to be touched and held and made to feel valued and special. Pedo was more than happy to provide all of these things in the sickest most vile way possible. Understandably, she mistook everything he said and did for love.

In later years, guilt and self-hatred stemming from the horrors of her childhood and the subsequent loss of her family would almost kill her.

PICTURE PERFECT

Soon enough Evil-lyn started adding lambs to the brood. Lamb 1 (a boy) came into their lives when Verity was three, Lamb 2 (another boy) arrived two years later and, finally, Lamb 3 (a girl) joined the dysfunctional troop one year after that. Verity loved them all as soon as she laid eyes on them and took her big sister duties seriously.

Evil-lyn and Pedo proceeded to paint the family as the neighbourhood gold standard for the ***Good Life***. They were both all about appearances. They lived well, they had a nice house (right beside Evil-lyn's parents), they had all the necessities of life, and more. They dressed the kids up nicely and put them all in sports. They attended Verity's figure skating competitions and her brothers' hockey and baseball games, and to the outside world they looked like a fun-loving, loud family who had it all.

Finally, one day, like the icing on a cake, Evil-lyn proudly displayed a large professionally done family portrait above the dining room table. They were all dressed in white, and their huge white smiles beamed out at the world. Sometimes Verity would stare up at the portrait and think, "What a beautiful picture. That's not *our* family; they must be actors pretending to be us." The abuse carried on, and the skeletons in the closet multiplied and gathered dust.

Evil-lyn was never real. The face and the character she presented to her friends and the world at large was fake, as if plastic surgery had been done on her soul. She was materialistic and loved to have nice things, to be the centre of attention and the envy of her friends. She never cooked. Dinner was always take-out or frozen prepared food, and the house was spotless.

Pedo was the funny guy, the nice guy, the guy who would always lend a hand, the guy who loved kids. Verity's maternal grandparents loved him, as did Evil-lyn's younger sister and later on, her husband. It was like Pedo too had cosmetic surgery on his personality, like he was altered to look like the best dad ever, when underneath his real pedophile self was lurking. In much the same way that cosmetic surgery doesn't last and has to be redone many times until the face no longer resembles its original state, the soul or personality suffers the same fate. An ugly distorted version eventually emerges, and everyone can finally see that the personality that everyone saw was never real, that all along it had simply been a desperate attempt to hide who the person really was.

When Verity was six, her parents announced that she was a "big girl" and she should sleep in her own bed. As Verity got older it became more difficult for Pedo to carry out the nightly molestations with Evil-lyn in the same bed. When Verity moved into her own bed, he was able to molest her early in the morning after her mother went to work and again in the middle of the night. Like a good teacher he gave her hands-on lessons in how to give him pleasure, and he withheld her pleasure until he was satisfied.

Pedo always told Verity that he loved her more than anyone else in his life, including her mother. He was a master groomer, and he knew how to manipulate her body and soul. Even though she loved him like her daddy, she also felt like she was in an adult relationship with him, his mistress. He would tell her over and over that the only reason he stayed in their home was because he loved ***her***, and he couldn't stand the thought of being away from her. Verity was terrified that he might leave, and her anxiety grew and festered like an open wound.

TARNISHED MEMORIES

One beautiful spring day when Verity was seven, Pedo brought home a little pink bicycle with a banana seat. Verity was so excited; she couldn't wait to ride it. "Come on, I'll teach you how to ride it," Pedo said as she chased him out onto the street. Verity's maternal grandparents and her mother watched happily as Pedo scooped her up onto the banana seat and began pushing her down the street. He put one hand on the handlebar and placed his other hand under the side of her bum pushing two of his fingers inside of her. Evil-lyn and Grandma and Grandpa smiled and clapped every time Pedo and Verity went by and every time they went by Verity would look directly into Evil-lyn's eyes. *Why aren't you stopping this? Don't you see what he's doing?*

By this time Verity was starting to figure out that the things Pedo was doing to her were wrong somehow. She couldn't bear the thought of him stopping, but feelings of guilt were beginning to niggle away at the corners of her mind and in the pit of her stomach. She had no idea why or what to do about it; she just knew that it didn't feel right anymore. Still, she reasoned that it must be okay. No one seemed angry with her or with Pedo for what they were doing or showed any signs that they even cared. In reality, her mother was more than "okay" with it. She encouraged it with her silence and indifference, sitting passively on the sidelines letting her daughter be used as a sex toy by her husband.

Once again, what should have been a happy milestone in Verity's little girl life was tarnished and ugly from that day on. It became one of many memories that would trigger anxiety and depression for the rest of her life.

MOMMY'S LITTLE HELPER

When Verity was about eight years old, Evil-lyn began giving her chores to do. She loved her little brothers and her baby sister, so she was happy to help out—changing diapers, cleaning up after them, and making sure they ate every day. She never had to cook meals because they never ate anything home-cooked; however, cleaning up after four kids and two adults was no easy task. Evil-lyn was a cruel boss with OCD tendencies, so if everything wasn't done to her standards, which were pretty much impossible to live up to, especially for an eight-year-old girl, she would yell at Verity, pull her hair, hit her, and kick her. Evil-lyn was smart though, smart enough to land her kicks and slaps on parts of the body that weren't exposed to the public. Sometimes Verity would wonder if clumps of her hair would be yanked from her scalp or if she would throw up from the kicks to her stomach.

The only parental love the little girl ever felt came from Pedo and the sick, twisted sexual existence that she had absolutely no control over. At times Verity could feel a pure dark hatred that she couldn't understand exuding from her mother. She believed Pedo loved her, so when he never intervened and tried to stop the abuse she was puzzled and hurt. *Why doesn't he stop her from hurting me? He loves me; he tells me all the time. He must be afraid of her too. After all, she calls him names and yells at him too,* Verity would reason. Regardless of his reasons, he never stepped in. He just walked away—until one day, to Verity's short-lived relief, he did attempt a half-hearted offense on her behalf.

As always, Verity could hear them arguing from her room in the basement. Pedo's voice was low and weak. "I think you should take it a bit easier on her, that's all, before you really hurt her."

"I think ***you*** should mind your own fucking business. You're getting what you want aren't you? What you're doing is a lot worse than what I'm doing. You're such a fucking joke," Evil-lyn screamed at Pedo, and as usual, he quietly backed down. That was the day that Verity started to come to the realization that as much as she didn't want to believe it, her mother did know what was going on. The seeds of doubt were planted, and there was no going back to her precious oblivion. Little did she know, life was about to get even harder.

A SECRET LIFE

Life carried on for Verity. She never mentioned anything about what was going on at home to the little girls at school, her teachers, or anyone else. Her classmates had such nice moms and dads. She would watch longingly as their parents hugged and kissed their little girls. She couldn't imagine ***those*** moms ever hitting or kicking ***their*** little girls. Then again, Evil-lyn looked just like those moms when she was in public. Verity thought, even hoped, that maybe the other girls' dads did the same things to them as Pedo did to her because that would mean it was okay and normal. But something always told her that this was not the case and stopped her from talking about it. Somewhere deep inside she knew that what was happening to her wasn't normal, and it wasn't okay. When she thought about it too much her stomach felt sick, and she would run a bath and scrub her private parts over and over again, a behavior that kept up well into adulthood.

One day Verity arrived at school to find her best friend surrounded by a few of their other friends. The girls were laughing out loud, obviously thoroughly enjoying her best friend's account of some funny story. Verity was anxious to join the group and find out what all the laughter was about. She hurried over to the group and pushed her way into the circle asking, "What's so funny?" Her best friend looked at her with a little smile, the kind of half smile you have when you're caught gossiping and you know it's wrong.

"I was just telling them about what happened when your daddy asked me to sit on his knee, and his penis got all hard."

Verity was horrified. Her eyes started to water but she quickly gained her composure and laughed it off. "Oh that, that was so funny, eh?" At eight years old she was already adept at hiding her emotions. She and the other girls giggled some more before the school bell prompted them all to go inside.

By this time Pedo had begun telling her never to tell anyone, warning her that they would stop him from making her feel good, that they would both be in a lot of trouble, and that he would have to leave. He would always follow his warnings with assurance that he loved her more than anyone and that what they were doing was okay, it just had to be their secret. Verity loved him, and she couldn't bear the thought of his leaving. She was fully addicted to the orgasms and to his so called "love" for her. Sometimes she would lie awake at night thinking about losing him, and many scenarios would come to mind. *I would be here all alone, and mom would hurt me even more. Daddy wouldn't make me feel good anymore, I wouldn't see him anymore, everyone would blame me . . .* Worries and fears swirled round and round in her mind, causing anxiety that no little girl should have to live with. This was the beginning of a lifelong mental illness that Verity would battle for the rest of her life.

I LOVE YOU MORE

By the time Verity was eight, Pedo was coming to her room almost every morning and every night. If she thought for any reason that he might not come, she would use what she thought of as their secret code and whisper, "I'm sleeping naked tonight, Daddy." She was hopelessly infatuated with him and how he made her feel, even though the feelings of guilt and self-loathing were growing and starting to eat away at her soul. Like any addiction, it had to be fed, and the more she fed it, the more addicted she became. It was wrong. She grew more and more sure of this every day. But the addiction to him and what he was doing to her was more powerful than any feelings of guilt or shame.

"I don't want to be with Mommy anymore. Verity, I don't love her. I love you more that anyone in the world. But if I leave, I won't get to see you anymore. No one loves you as much as I do, you know that, right?" His words made her feel so loved and needed but at the same time struck such fear in her heart. She was terrified that he would leave, and the only adult who truly loved her would be gone.

Right around this time Pedo decided Verity was "ready" and *he* told her as much one morning while he was molesting her. Verity thought about this all day long and wondered what he meant. *Ready for what?* Whatever it was, she wasn't afraid. In fact, she looked forward to the surprise in much the same way that a little girl might anxiously await a treat that her daddy promised to bring home for her after work.

Her eight-year-old brain reasoned that everything he had been doing to her for as long as she could remember felt so good that this could only be better. *I can't wait. What is he going to do to me?*

That night he raped her for the first time. He was careful to make sure no physical damage was done and, as usual, he assured her that he loved her and reminded her that their secret had to stay a secret if she wanted him to stay living with her. She would have done anything to ensure he didn't move out. After all, he was staying there just for her. He was doing *everything* for *her*; only she could make him happy. Her little girl life was now a complete sham, a living hell. Pedo was using her for sex almost every day. She was conflicted and confused and always worried, yet she felt like he was the only one who loved her.

WHO KNEW?

All throughout Verity's childhood she was close to her mother's family. Her maternal grandparents lived next door, so a quick scoot across the backyard when she was old enough to go alone was common. Her maternal aunt also lived close by. They all spent a lot of time together. Birthdays, Thanksgiving, Christmas, and Easter were family events. It wasn't unusual for Verity to run across the backyard to spend time with her grandparents to avoid a beating if her mother was having a meltdown. There were other times, after she began to want Pedo's abuse to stop, that she would curl up on the couch at their house just to be out of his reach.

Her grandmother was more comfortable showing affection with hugs than her grandfather was. He would play silly little games with her to make her laugh, and she understood that this was his way of showing affection. It wasn't unusual for her grandmother to take her shopping, just the two of them, spending time together laughing and looking at clothes. Verity was their first grandchild, after all, and although it didn't feel like the intense all-consuming love that Pedo showed her, it still felt nice and warm and easy. She could be herself there; she didn't have to do adult chores or perform adult sexual favours. She could pretend life was normal and she was just like any other little girl visiting her grandma and grandpa.

Verity was also close to her maternal aunt. Her aunt was eight years younger than Evil-lyn, and she treated Verity more like a little sister than a niece. It was fun to spend time with her, do girl stuff, and talk about boys. It was her aunt's home that Verity ran to as a teenager when her parents kicked her out.

Sadly, no one made her feel loved *enough* or safe *enough* to share with them what Pedo was doing to her. When she grew up, she came to believe that many of them knew what was going on, but they were weak and simply didn't want anything, especially this sick secret, to upset their lives or show the world the disease that was festering under their noses. In hindsight there were obvious signs that they *did* know what was going on. When this revelation crept into Verity's mind as an adult, it was one of the hardest things she ever had to come to terms with.

RAIN DAYS

Verity opened her eyes and stretched. Rain was pouring down, hitting her window with loud splats. The realization that it was a rain day hit her, and she immediately jumped up wanting to get ready for school and out the door before Pedo could stop her. Her mother had already gone to work. Verity pulled her clothes on, quickly ran a brush through her bed head hair, swished some mouth wash around her mouth, and crept up the stairs to the front door, grabbing her school bag and raincoat on the way out. The only good thing about rain days was that Pedo would be busy getting her little brothers and sister ready for school, so he wouldn't notice her leaving until she was already out the door. "Bye, see you later," Verity called out as she ran to the bus stop.

She hated rain days. Rain days meant that Pedo—who owned his own roofing company—would be home all day and that he would keep her home and rape and molest her all day long. She was ten by this time, and although she was still very much addicted to Pedo and their private activities, like any addict, she wanted it to stop. She wanted to be free of it.

Around lunchtime on one such day, Verity lay on Pedo's bed watching the rain hit the window like large tear drops. Sadness and shame enveloped her, and she wondered, as she often did, if her life would ever be normal. Pedo had gone to the kitchen to get a drink, instructing Verity to "stay right there" when suddenly he burst back into the bedroom in a panic. He peered outside from behind the curtains. "Be quiet and get downstairs," he said. Verity grabbed her clothes from the floor and ran for the stairs, wondering what could possibly be wrong. Pedo practically pushed her down the stairs, hissing at her to stay in her room until he called her. A couple of minutes passed, and she heard the front door open and close. She recognized her grandparents' voices chatting away with Pedo about work and the weather. In her mind she screamed at them, *Don't you see my shoes and my school bag right there by the door? I'm down here, ask him why I'm not at school!* They made it so easy for him.

CINDERELLA WITH A TWIST

It was the middle of the night when Evil-lyn showed up at Verity's bedroom door, presumably looking for Pedo. The door creaked open, and Pedo froze on top of Verity. She stood there surveying the scene before her for what felt to Verity like an eternity. Pedo quickly turned his face away from the light. Verity held her breath, transfixed by the silhouette of her mother in the doorway. Evil-lyn looked directly at them then turned, closed the door, and walked back upstairs without saying a word or showing any hint of emotion. Tears welled up in Verity's eyes and rolled down the side of her face onto her pillow. *She knows but she doesn't care.* She's never going to save me, no one is.

Verity was partly right. Evil-lyn did know, and she was not going to save her. She care, just not about Verity. Verity was about to learn about an age-old emotion—jealousy. The little girl had never felt any love from her mother, but she could now feel even more blatant disgust almost every time her mother looked at her. Sometimes Verity would turn around from whatever she was doing and find her mother glaring at her. She was a "whore" now, and her mother had no problem calling her that every chance she got.

After that night things got even worse with Evil-lyn. The physical abuse was more frequent, and Verity's list of chores grew. Verity's mother was rarely even slightly nice to her anymore. "You're a fat and lazy little bitch," she would scream at her, no matter how hard she tried to please her. Evil-lyn started to make a point of talking dirty to Pedo in front ofVerity, insisting that he return the banter.

One night after Pedo left her bed, Verity curled up naked with the blankets pulled up over her head. His smell was all around her like a noxious gas threatening to turn her stomach, so she quickly pulled the blankets down. Apparently Pedo had unwittingly woken up Evil-lyn when he crawled back into their bed like a snake. She could hear Evil-lyn yelling at him, "What the fuck are you doing? If you can't stay in our bed, don't come in here waking me up in the middle of the night!" More proof, if she needed it, that Evil-lyn knew exactly what was going on.

The next morning Evil-lyn stomped down the basement stairs and pushed Verity's bedroom door open so hard that it bounced back, almost hitting her in the face. "Get up and get dressed and get your fucking chores done."

Verity sat up, trying to hold back the tears because tears only infuriated Evil-lyn more. She knew the beatings weren't going to stop. In fact, they would probably get worse.

It was Saturday so she spent some time playing with Lamb 1 and Lamb 2, and then her favourite—her little baby sister, Lamb 3. "I love you little one. We're going to be best friends forever. I'll do your hair, and we'll go shopping for clothes and share them, and I'll keep you safe, always." Verity breathed in the smell of Lamb 3's white-blonde hair and kissed her chubby cheeks—a ray of sunshine in Verity's dreary life.

THE COMPETITION

One Saturday morning when Verity was twelve it became clear to her that not only did her mother hate her, but she believed that her mother was in some secret sick competition with her.

It was a sunny and warm June day. Verity was lying on the sofa with her back flat on the cushions and her legs draped over one arm, half watching something on TV. Pedo and Evil-lyn were in the kitchen in the next room making an unusual, for them, happy ruckus. Verity was pulled out of her partial daydream by the sound of them laughing, jostling each other around, and bumping into things. She sat up wondering what could be going on just as they fell into the living room, Evil-lyn pulling a guilty-looking, protesting Pedo with her. Pedo was laughing, but it was clear he was uncomfortable with the whole situation, like he was flirting with Evil-lyn in front of his girlfriend or something. Evil-lyn, on the other hand, was thoroughly enjoying the performance. She laughed loudly, looked directly at Verity and grabbed Pedo's crotch. She playfully pulled Pedo toward the bathroom and shouted back to Verity, "We're going in the shower for some adult time; you know what I mean, right?" The bathroom door was left open, and Verity could clearly hear them having sex. As much as she wanted to tear herself away from the sounds of what was happening, she couldn't. Her stomach felt sick, and her head hurt. When the show finally ended and they emerged from the bathroom, her mother stark naked and Pedo with a towel around his waist, Verity was frozen in place not knowing what to say or do. It was clear, even in her twelve-year-old mind, that her mother had set the whole thing up to make her jealous—to put her in her place and prove to her that Pedo was not hers and that Verity was no competition for her mother. Evil-lyn glared at her. "Clean up the bathroom. We made a bit of a mess in there," she ordered triumphantly. Pedo hung his head and followed her sheepishly down the hallway toward their bedroom.

ALL IN THE FAMILY

"Hey are you awake? Push over and let me in," Verity whispered. Her younger brother, Lamb 1, was half asleep, but he moved over and let her crawl in beside him.

A few months earlier he had the misfortune to walk in on Pedo raping his sister. It left an uneasy feeling in his stomach. He knew that what he witnessed was bad and dark and wrong, and every time he thought about it afterward it would replay in his mind like a scary movie. He could hear his father's unusually harsh half whisper half yell, "Get the fuck out of here! What the fuck are doing in here? Get out now!"

Lamb 1 sat up rubbing his eyes. "What are you doing here? What's the matter?"

"I heard him coming downstairs so I ran in here. I don't want him doing things to me anymore. I hate it but I can't say no once he starts." Verity curled up in a ball and pretended she was asleep. She could hear Pedo approaching the door, so she squeezed her eyes shut and whispered, "Pretend you're sleeping." The door squeaked open and Pedo's silhouette loomed in the doorway for what felt like forever, then he turned and headed back upstairs.

Lamb 1 nudged her in the back with his elbow. "He's gone, get up."

Verity turned around and faced Lamb 1. "Can I sleep in here with you? He might come back down."

"Does it hurt? What he does to you, does it hurt?" Lamb 1 asked.

Verity was excited to be able to talk to someone about what Pedo was doing to her. She had never told a soul, never shared how she felt about it or how she felt about him. She trusted Lamb 1. After all he was her little brother and they loved each other. Verity propped her head up on her elbow and peered into Lamb 1's face. A shaft of yellow light shone in through a crack in the doorway and she could see honest interest on his face.

"It doesn't hurt. It actually feels good—so good that I can't say no to him. He does things to me, and he makes me do things to him."

Lamb 1 stared at her. "Why don't you like it?"

"I do like the feeling, but I feel gross when he's done. I don't want to do it anymore, but I'm afraid he'll move out if I stop. He says he will." Tears started to well up in Verity's eyes. She could tell that Lamb 1 was having a hard time understanding the whole thing, and now she was terrified that he would tell someone or worse, he would turn against her and think she was gross and slutty. Verity was well aware that she really had no one except Pedo and her siblings, and she was terrified that she might have said too much.

"I don't get it." Lamb 1 was sitting up now, his interest peaked. "Show me."

Verity was taken aback. She didn't want to do *sex stuff* with her little brother, but sex and love were all mixed up in her mind, and as it was now part of her personality, she had a really hard time saying no. "I don't want to Lamb 1; it's gross."

They were around nine and eleven when it began, and almost two years passed before it stopped. Verity felt dirty and "gross" after every incident but was always able to justify their actions by calling it love. That's what love meant to her. It felt wrong and right at the same time, and Verity was again caught in a downward spiral, this time with her little brother. The nuances of childhood—baseball, hockey, figure skating, swimming and summer games of tag—were now all tangled together with sex in the sick reality that was her life.

THE GIFT

Verity eased herself into the bathtub full of warm water and relieved herself. For the past few days, she couldn't bear the intense burning that came with going to pee in the toilet, but she discovered that peeing in the water while she was submersed in the tub eased the pain. She also noticed that there was some kind of discharge in her underwear, and it smelled bad. She was thirteen years old, and unbeknownst to her, Pedo had given her a gift—an STD.

After a week she decided that as much as she dreaded it, she had to ask Evil-lyn to take her to the doctor. "Mom, I think I need to go to the doctor."

"What the hell now Verity?" Evil-lyn snarled.

"It burns so bad when I pee that I have to pee in the bathtub, and it smells really bad down there." Verity put her head down; she really didn't want to do this.

"You know what? That's fucking disgusting. You're disgusting. I'm not taking you to the doctor. You can get the fuck out of my sight. You make me sick."

Verity went to her room and sat on her bed wondering what she was going to do. She still didn't know what exactly was causing her symptoms, but she knew it had something to do with Pedo, and she knew that was why Evil-lyn was so mad at her. *What am I going to do? I can't tell anyone. What if I get really sick and die? I don't even care. Mom sure wouldn't care.* Tears ran down her cheeks. She pulled her legs up to her chest and curled up in her bed hoping that she would fall asleep and not wake up or, even better, she would wake up in a new home with a new family, a family with a mom who loved her and a dad who didn't ask her to do gross things that were becoming harder and harder for her to do.

Verity went to school all the next week hoping and praying that no one could smell the discharge. She bathed at least twice a day and tried to drink as little as possible because it was so excruciating to pee without being in the bath. By midweek the discharge had lessened and the burning sensation had eased significantly. Pedo hadn't come to her room since she told Evil-lyn about her problem. Even though on the one hand it was a relief, on the other hand she started to feel anxious and worried that he didn't love her anymore. After all, aside from her little brothers and sister, Pedo was the only person who showed her any physical affection or ever told her that he loved her.

After dinner on Friday evening, Evil-lyn approached Verity. They were alone in the kitchen and Verity was cleaning up the mess on the floor around the table. "So, does it still hurt when you go to the bathroom? Is there still a bad smell?" Evil-lyn stood leaning on the stove waiting for Verity's answer.

It felt good to have Evil-lyn show some interest and concern, and Verity was eager to share something, anything, with her mother. "There's no more pain, and the smell is gone too." Her good feeling didn't last long.

"Well, you're lucky it wasn't a whole lot worse. That's what happens to little whores. And I will tell you this much, you won't be bringing home a baby for me to raise. You're going to the doctor to get birth control pills tomorrow morning, and don't bother telling him anything about the gross disease you picked up." Evil-lyn turned on her heel and left the kitchen without another word.

Verity stood in the middle of the dining room trying to understand what had just happened. *What the fuck?? I haven't been with anyone except your husband,* Verity silently screamed at her. *But you know that, don't you? That's why I have to get birth control, so I won't get pregnant with your husband's baby.*

Later that day, Verity sat on the basement stairs thinking about her shitty life. *Why me? Why do I have to have such a bitch for a mother and pedophile for a father? Well, fuck her, I am not gonna take her shit anymore!*

Almost on cue, Evil-lyn appeared beside her, looking down at her with the usual disgust on her face. Her face changed immediately whenever she looked at Verity. She could be happy and smiling and laughing, but whenever Verity entered the room, a darkness would settle over her like the Grim Reaper's cloak.

"Get off of the stairs, Stupid. Somebody will trip over you."

"Well, maybe it will be you, bitch!"

Evil-lyn pulled Verity's arm back and landed a resounding slap on her cheek. Verity cupped her hand over her cheek feeling the heat from the welt while Evil-lyn angrily made her way down the rest of the stairs into the basement.

It hurt physically, but that didn't dampen the feeling that she had actually won something, that she had made a point. She had fought back.

Pedo returned to her bed that night. She didn't want him there, and she told him so, turning her back on him and curling up into a ball. But, as usual, he begged and pleaded and told her that he loved her and missed her, and she gave in . . . again. Afterwards she lay in the dark hating herself and planning another life, a better life, a normal life, a life where someone would love her without asking for anything in return, especially sex. Little did she know that no matter how hard she tried, she would mistake sex for love for many years to come and that her addiction to sex would feed her addiction to drugs. Nevertheless, in that moment, it felt good to dream and hope.

The next morning there was a five-dollar bill lying on her dresser. She picked it up and stood looking at for a few minutes like she was trying to identify a foreign object. She soon figured out exactly what it meant. She had begun to refuse Pedo more and more often, and this was his way of paying her for her service, knowing that few adolescent girls will refuse some spending money. Sometimes he would leave five dollars, sometimes ten. It always left a sick feeling in the pit of her stomach when she stuffed it into her school bag. *Huh, I guess I really am a whore now. Well, whatever, fuck him.*

A WAY OUT?

Not too long after Verity and Lamb 1 started doing *sex stuff* together, Lamb 1 began to act out at school. He was fighting, skipping class, and talking back to the teachers. He was angry and out of control, and Verity couldn't think of any way to help him. She hated seeing him this way; she knew how he felt. They talked, but never about what the two of them were doing when they were alone together. She wanted to stop, and she was sure he did too, but they were both caught up in the web that Pedo and Evil-lyn had spun, and like flies, they were hopelessly trapped.

Pedo and Evil-lyn were pulled into parent/teacher meetings almost weekly. The school pushed them to enroll all of the children in school counselling. They feigned bewilderment and concern, all the while assuring the teachers that they couldn't understand, or even imagine, what could be going on with Lamb 1, and "rest assured, we will do everything we can to help get to the bottom of this, whatever it takes." They managed to avoid counselling by stalling and giving Oscar-winning performances as the best parents ever. Verity begged and pleaded to be allowed to go to counselling. In the back of her mind, although she never *planned* to give away their dirty family secrets, she knew it would be good for her *and* for her siblings and maybe, just maybe, it was their way out.

In the end, the counselling never happened. Pedo and Evil-lyn argued about it daily. Oddly, Pedo was beginning to cave, but Evil-lyn would have none of it. "Are you fucking crazy? They'll dig until they find out everything! They'll pick us apart! No!" As usual, Pedo backed down, the kids were pulled out of the school and enrolled in a Catholic school, which didn't push so hard for school counselling, and just like that, the window to help that Verity had been praying for was slammed shut.

HER SISTER'S KEEPER

When Verity was around fourteen, the abuse stopped. It seemed like two things happened. One, she was finally able to stick to her guns and refuse to have sex with Pedo, and two, he strangely began to lose interest in her. Verity was pleased; it felt like it was finally over. Of course, in reality her ordeal was far from over, and the repercussions of her childhood trauma would be something she would battle for the rest of her life.

One day, out of the blue, it hit her. *If he isn't after me anymore, who* is *he after?* Even at fifteen she wasn't naïve enough to think that Pedo miraculously overcame pedophilia and was going to be a model husband and father from here on.

He had taken to being rude and inappropriate with her, pointing out her weight, accusing her of being a slut, and insinuating she was stupid. He and Evil-lyn were a team now, and they would gang up on her, verbally abusing and making fun of her. This hurt more that Verity wanted to admit, even to herself. After all, even though she now fully understood that what he had been doing to her was wrong in every way, she still couldn't let go of the belief that he loved her. And what somehow felt even worse was knowing that she still loved him.

Verity would watch him with her little sister, looking for any signs that he was abusing her. She watched closely with the keen eyes of someone who had been there and experienced those touches under the blanket while they were watching a movie, the whispers when others were out of earshot, and having money to go to the store when the other kids had none. Nothing stood out, but she couldn't shake the feeling that if it hadn't started already, it could start any day, and she was the only one who could stop it.

She took to sleeping with her sister to ensure that he didn't sneak into her bed at night or early in the morning. Lamb 3 was more than happy to go along with this, loving the time they spent together giggling, discussing hair and clothes, cuddling, and just being sisters.

Lamb 3 always maintained that Pedo never touched her. In a statement to the judge when she was sixteen, she swore that her father never abused her. Verity always hoped and prayed that this was true because no matter how hurt she was by her family calling her a liar and abandoning her (after she charged Pedo), she loved them all, especially her baby sister.

ENOUGH

Life carries on regardless of the horrors hiding behind the outward appearance of goodness. So it was with Verity's life. From the outside looking in, her life was normal. It was noisy and busy and messy, and aside from the occasional bump in the road, such as notes sent home from school for skipping, and the kids missing their curfew, it was, outwardly normal. Inside, however, the disease flourished, as it does with any untreated infection.

Verity began using cocaine at a party when she was fifteen. She loved it immediately. It was like a switch had been flipped, and she just felt *good*, plain and simple. When she was high, she had a happy energy about her, and her fucked-up childhood wasn't such a big deal. Soon afterwards, Lamb 1 jumped on the cocaine wagon with her at a party, and he too was immediately hooked on the false euphoria. It was an outlet for them both. They could finally talk about what happened between them, and although their deep conversations were artificially produced and directed by cocaine, it felt like the perfect solution at the time.

Verity had boyfriends, and she had no qualms about having sex with them. In her mind, sex was a natural normal way to show affection, and it was really no big deal. Besides, she *needed* it. She just didn't want to get it from Pedo anymore. He had been her dealer, so to speak, and she wanted a new dealer.

The more she refused Pedo, the more rude he became. Partying and using cocaine was a happy distraction, and she craved distraction. Evil-lyn was more than happy to feed the rift between Pedo and Verity, so every day began and ended with a screaming match between Evil-lyn and her "whore" daughter.

No matter how dysfunctional and warped her family life was underneath, Verity really did love her brothers and sister, and she especially loved watching Lamb 1 play hockey. One evening in January when she was around fifteen, she was eagerly looking forward to one such game. She quickly got ready in her room, which was in the basement, and bounded up the stairs to make sure she was ready to go on time.

Pedo stood by the kitchen sink looking out the window. "What are you all dressed up for?"

Verity laughed a little thinking he must be joking. "The game, of course."

"Nope, you're sitting this one out. You have chores and homework to do, don't you?"

Verity started to think that maybe he wasn't joking after all. "I'll do everything when I get back."

Pedo had become increasingly rude and openly mean ever since she started refusing him sex, and today was no exception. "No, you'll do everything while *we're* at the game."

Anger was boiling up inside Verity now. "If you don't let me go to the game, I'll tell everyone what you've been doing to me!"

Much to her surprise, Pedo didn't appear to be the least bit concerned about her threat. "Really? You are just as much to blame, and you know it. You enjoyed it! Didn't you keep asking for it? Go ahead and tell whoever you want; we'll see who they blame."

Pedo turned around and headed outside to the waiting van full of boisterous excited kids, slamming the door on his way out.

Verity stood at the top of the basement stairs. She was defeated. All the happiness and anticipation she felt leading up to this evening drained out of her. *He's right. I did enjoy it, and I did ask for it.* She had kept the notion of threatening him stored at the back of her brain like her ace in the hole. As it turned out, he had a better hand.

Now, feeling trapped and defeated, she became steadily more angry and more defiant with each passing day. One evening she returned home after school to find her belongings on the front lawn. It was clear that her mother had never wanted her there, and now that she wasn't of any use to Pedo, he would rather she were gone. She picked her things up, crying as she went, and resigned herself to the fact that no one really loved her, not real unconditional love, at least. Love from the people in her life was totally conditional and totally fake. *Maybe it's me; maybe I'm just unlovable.*

A NEW CHAPTER

Verity showed up at her aunt's house with her suitcase, and for a time it was fun, like an extended girls' sleepover. But her addiction needed to be fed, and she soon moved in with a new boyfriend. Life was a series of parties, playing house, and feeding her insatiable hunger for sex and cocaine. In spite of everything, she missed her family, all of them. One weekend she mustered up the courage to go home for a visit. She was ecstatic to see her little brothers and sister. She was even happy to see her mother who, for whatever reason, didn't seem to hate her quite as much as before. Her happiness was short lived. Before she could escape back to the relative safety of her aunt's, Pedo happened again. He cajoled his way back in, using all his old tools—her hatred of herself, her lack of self-worth, and finally, plain old loneliness. Afterward Verity felt sick with guilt and shame. She had failed; she had promised herself that this would never happen again. She felt weak and pathetic. Her addiction to sex and to him had allowed her to let her guard down and be conned by his bullshit, yet again.

Somehow, she managed to graduate from high school in spite of the parties and drug use that she used as tools to bury memories and feelings about her childhood. Pride, however, was not a feeling that she had ever been familiar with, so her graduation was nothing more than a legitimate reason to party.

AWAKENING

Verity's childhood had been filled with parties, family get-togethers, figure skating, hockey and baseball games. Pedo and Evil-lyn were social butterflies, and family and friends would stop by all the time, not just to visit but to leave their children with Pedo to babysit on his days off.

As it turned out Pedo was sexually molesting many of the little girls he so happily babysat. He was a master at hiding what he was doing, even from Verity. One of his favourite games to play with them was hide-and-seek. He would help the little girls find places to hide, hide with them to keep them quiet, and sexually molest them while they waited. Verity didn't learn any of this until many years later.

By the time Verity was twenty-one, she was struggling with serious addictions to drugs and sex. She used her addictions to mute her inner voice, the tiny voice that wouldn't let up that kept telling her that Pedo needed to be stopped and that it was her responsibility to stop him.

One afternoon Verity stopped by her parents' house for a visit, hoping at least some of her siblings would be home. Pedo's truck was in the driveway, but her mother's car was gone. Verity considered the fact that he could be there alone, and that would once again put her in a position she never wanted to be in again. Even in her twenties she knew she couldn't trust herself to say no to him. She sat in her car weighing how much she wanted to see her brothers and sister against how much she didn't want to be alone with Pedo. In the end, she decided to *put on her big girl pants* and pushed open the front door. The house seemed almost eerily quiet. She stood in the entryway wondering where everyone could be at this time of day. Something told her not to call out, so she quietly walked down the basement stairs. When she entered the rec room the scene before *her* took her breath away, and she froze on the spot, unable to breath or even move her legs to leave.

Pedo lay on the sofa spooning Verity's five-year-old cousin. Both the little girl and Pedo were sleeping soundly, their breath synchronized. A little droplet of drool threatened to drip from the little girl's partly opened mouth onto the back of the chubby hand she had tucked under her cheek. Verity was suddenly hit with a vivid flash back—Pedo in her bed wrapped around ***her*** at this same age, his beard stubble scratching the side of her face and his hot breath in her ear. She stumbled backward a few steps, finally managing to gain control of her legs before she tripped. She turned and ran back up the stairs, not caring if she woke them or not, just wanting out, wanting to get far away from the scene so she could *breathe and think*. She jumped in her car and sped down the street, pulling down a dirt side road and coming to a halt in front of an abandoned barn.

I have to stop him; this is not just about me. If he hurts anyone else, it's on me—I am letting it happen! Tears rolled down Verity's cheeks. All the excuses she had been able to come up with to convince herself that she didn't have to report him seemed feeble and weak now in light of what she had just witnessed.

Everything that her future husband, then boyfriend, had been telling her ever since she told him about what had happened to her as a child made sense now. He had urged her to report Pedo and said that he would no longer allow their baby boy to be babysat by Pedo or Evil-lyn.

At first Verity couldn't comprehend how their eighteen-month-old son could be at risk around her parents; Pedo wasn't interested in boys. She was now beginning to understand the term *Generational* Trauma—how something as seemingly insignificant as ignoring what a pedophile and his/her supporters have done, pretending it didn't happen, can do serious damage to everyone involved for generations to come.

If I don't go to the police, I am teaching my son that what Pedo did was okay and, as a result, he might allow someone to do that to him or his children, and the cycle will never stop. Verity mulled all of this over in her mind.

A week later, with the support of her boyfriend, members of his family, her mother's sister, her maternal grandparents, and Pedo's father and stepmother, Verity reported Pedo to the police. In her account of what he did to her, she stopped short of telling them that he raped her. She shared only the sexual molestation and how long it went on. She couldn't bring herself to say he raped her; it was too painful and humiliating. Shortly thereafter, five other women came forward with reports of child sexual abuse at the hands of Pedo, and charges were filed against him. Pedo was convicted on all counts and sentenced to four and a half years in a federal prison. Unfortunately, he served less than two years behind bars. Upon his release he was allowed to be with his grandchildren under the supervision of Evil-lyn—the very person who allowed the abuse to happen to Verity and her friends, the person who stayed married to the man who sexually abused her own baby girl.

Her mother and her siblings never spoke to her after Pedo was charged, except to call her a liar and to harass and threaten her. Her aunt staunchly supported her, knowing that he quite likely abused her daughters too. Sadly, when Verity was thirty-four, more than ten years after Pedo's conviction, her aunt and her maternal grandparents abruptly decided that they wanted to repair their relationship with Pedo and Evil-lyn and tried to convince Verity that she too should "let it all go" and reunite with her family.

Verity was astounded. Her aunt had been one of her greatest allies through everything, and although her grandparents had not been as vocal or outwardly supportive, they had stood by her and had stopped all contact with Evil-lyn and Pedo and even with their grandchildren. Now she felt hurt, betrayed, and abandoned all over again. How could they do this, knowing what they knew? She tried to explain her point of view to them. She tried to explain the message that this would send to her sons, to all the children Pedo abused, and to abused children in general. She tried to explain the risk she would be taking with her own mental health if she subjected herself to that toxicity again. She tried to explain her fear that she would start using IV drugs again. It all fell on deaf ears, and incredibly, they began to blame her and accuse her of "exaggerating" the severity of what happened to her.

Verity's heart was broken again, but she stood strong and refused to have any contact with her aunt and her grandparents if they were going to hang out with her abuser. It was harder than she could have ever imagined. More than once she came dangerously close to giving up and using again. She and her husband had been through hell and back, as had their sons, because of their serious drug addictions. They now had two years of sobriety under their belts and plans and goals for their family and their future.

I won't let them pull me in and abuse me, and now my children, all over again. I won't give up everything I have gained through hard work, she promised herself.

Today Verity runs an online support group that she started for children who have been, or are being, sexually abused. She has a podcast, and she plans to attend college. Her husband runs a successful business of his own, and he too is thankful for his recovery and the second chance at life they have been given. Clinton and Benji are beautiful, compassionate boys, and although they too are healing from the trauma of their parents' addiction, they know they are loved, and perhaps more importantly, they know that they are worthy and deserving of love.

HEALING

The sun is shining, and a light cool breeze is gently stirring the leaves in her backyard. It's Sunday morning, and Verity sits on the back deck, enjoying the warmth from the sun on her face. She loves Sundays. Sunday is family day, the day when her husband is home all day and they can all spend time together discussing the events of the week, good and bad. It is the day when she reflects on how far they have all come. She watches her husband wrestling with his boys, laughing, and giving them some tips on the ins and outs of "jits" (jujitsu). She can't help feeling that this is what it's all about, *this is happiness*.

Jimbo, their beloved dog, races around them, barking happily, wanting in on the fun. "C'mon boys. Let's take Jimbo for a walk," her husband yells. Off they go down the street, all three laughing and talking, Jimbo running ahead, urging them to hurry. She can hear Clinton, his quiet gentle voice always querying, always wondering about something. Benji picks up a stick and throws it for Jimbo.

They disappear around the corner, and her heart is filled with love—real love, the kind of love that doesn't hurt, the unconditional, honest, open kind of love she has *finally* been blessed with.

Still, some days are hard, days when her flashbacks are vivid and thoughts of using cross her mind. Whenever these thoughts creep into her mind, she steps back, regroups, is kind to herself, and reminds herself how far she has come and how thankful she is for the people in her life who love her and whom she loves. She is thankful that they found their path to recovery and that they found the strength to follow it before it was too late.

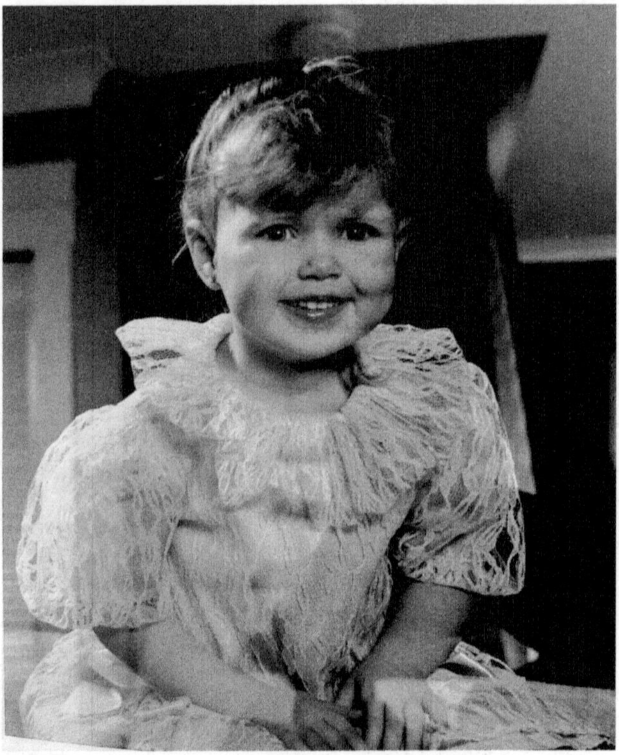

UPDATE JANUARY, 2023

Verity's abuser recently pled guilty to breaching the conditions laid out in his conviction as a registered child abuser. As a result, he was sentenced to only 3 months house arrest and 3 years probation.

It is our hope that anyone reading this will voice their concerns to their Members of Parliament (in Canada) and demand harsher penalties for convicted child abusers. Please help us stop child abuse, our children matter.

ABOUT THE AUTHOR

Rita Hamilton has a bachelor's degree both a double major in Sociology and Social Welfare and a minor in Psychology. She has 25 years of experience in the Social Service field, working with children and adults. She specializes in treatment of mental health and addiction problems that often stem from childhood trauma.

Rita collaborated with Tiffany Hamilton to create *Nobody's Baby* based on Tiffany's life. It is their hope that this book will foster greater understanding of childhood sexual abuse and the profound effects on survivors' lives.

Tiffany offers online support through her own online *Never Alone* support group, for survivors and current victims of child sexual abuse.

For more information, visit:
https://msha.ke/neveralone

Printed in Great Britain
by Amazon

19073460R00047